WHO MADE MY LUNCH?
FROM POTATO TO CHIP

BY MARI SCHUH • ILLUSTRATED BY JEANINE MURCH

AMICUS ILLUSTRATED is published by Amicus Learning, an imprint of Amicus
P.O. Box 227, Mankato, MN 56002
www.amicuspublishing.us

© 2025 Amicus. International copyright reserved in all countries. No part of this book may be reproduced in any form without written permission from the publisher.

LIBRARY OF CONGRESS CATALOGING-IN-PUBLICATION DATA
Names: Schuh, Mari C., 1975- author. | Murch, Jeanine Henderson, illustrator.
Title: From potato to chip / by Mari Schuh ; illustrated by Jeanine Murch.
Description: Mankato, MN : Amicus Illustrated is published by Amicus Learning, an imprint of Amicus, 2025. | Series: Who made my lunch? | Includes bibliographical references. | Audience: Ages 6-9 | Audience: Grades 2-3 | Summary: "A child wonders where potato chips come from and learns about the jobs of a potato farmer and food factory workers as they describe the steps in making potato chips. This illustrated narrative nonfiction book includes a world map of where potatoes are grown, glossary, and further resources, making it a great story to support farm-to-table education"—Provided by publisher.
Identifiers: LCCN 2024010619 (print) | LCCN 2024010620 (ebook) | ISBN 9798892001113 (library binding) | ISBN 9798892001694 (paperback) | ISBN 9798892002271 (ebook)
Subjects: LCSH: Potato chips—Juvenile literature. | Potato growers—Juvenile literature.
Classification: LCC TX803.P8 S38 2025 (print) | LCC TX803.P8 (ebook) | DDC 664/.80521—dc23/eng/20240402
LC record available at https://lccn.loc.gov/2024010619
LC ebook record available at https://lccn.loc.gov/2024010620

EDITOR: Rebecca Glaser
SERIES DESIGNER: Kathleen Petelinsek
BOOK DESIGNER: Kim Pfeffer

Printed in China

FOR ELLA AND MAX—M.S.

ABOUT THE AUTHOR
Mari Schuh's love of reading began with cereal boxes at the kitchen table. Today she is the author of hundreds of nonfiction books for beginning readers. She lives in the Midwest with her husband and their sassy house rabbit. Mari often enjoys buttery baked potatoes for dinner.

ABOUT THE ILLUSTRATOR
Jeanine Murch is an illustrator with a lifelong love of art, books, and storytelling. She lives in Pittsburgh, PA, with her husband, two children, and the world's most snuggly pup, all of which inspire her work. When she isn't making art, she's usually daydreaming about her next travel adventure.

Crunch! Potato chips are the perfect crunchy snack to put in your lunch. But what if you had to make the potato chips yourself? And you also had to grow the potatoes?

As a potato farmer, you'll want an area with warm days and cool nights. So pack your bags and move to Idaho! Idaho has rich soil. This helps make it the top state for growing potatoes.

In the spring, you'll plant pieces of seed potatoes. These small potatoes will grow into full potatoes underground.

Use a machine to build mounds of soil around each seed potato. The mounds keep sunlight from reaching the potatoes and turning them green. You don't want green potatoes!

In two to six weeks, you'll see plants growing. Soon, potatoes grow underground. Each plant can grow six to eight potatoes. Add fertilizer to the soil to help them grow.

Potatoes need soil that is moist but not soggy. Rain will help! But you'll also need to water your seed potatoes lightly and often. A sprinkler system works best.

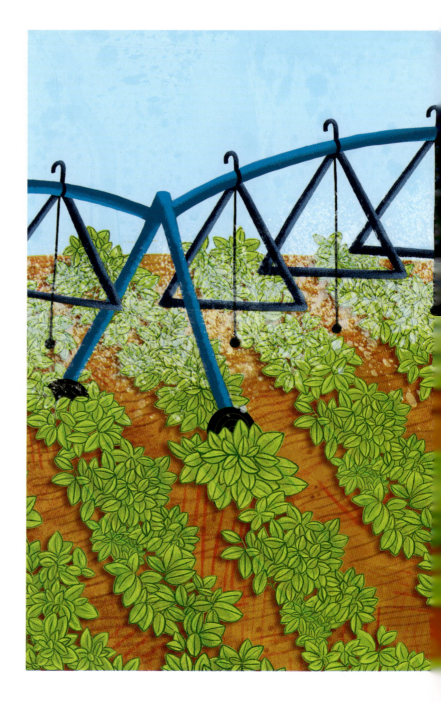

9

When fall comes, it is harvest time in Idaho. Pull a machine called a windrower behind your tractor to gently dig up your potatoes. The machine separates leaves, dirt, rocks, and potatoes. It puts the potatoes in rows on the ground.

Then pull a harvester behind your tractor. Your tractor's GPS system tells it exactly where to drive. The harvester picks up all the potatoes on the ground. It puts them into trucks. Soon the trucks are full!

Quick, deliver some potatoes to the potato chip factory that ordered them. The workers are ready!

Store the rest of the potatoes in storage buildings. Make sure the building has the right temperature, humidity, and air flow. Potatoes need to be kept in cool, dark buildings so they stay fresh.

At the factory, your potatoes travel on conveyor belts. First, workers get rid of rocks. Then the potatoes are dumped into water to get rid of smaller rocks. Next, machines with brushes clean the potatoes. No more dirt!

A machine peels the skin off the potatoes. Then a slicer quickly cuts the potatoes into thin slices.

Plop! The slices are dumped into big fryers full of oil. When they're done frying, a shaker adds salt and seasoning to the chips.

The chips are cooled and inspected by machines. A few workers taste some chips. Yum! The chips pass the taste test.

Factories are busy places. Some make thousands of pounds of potato chips an hour!

Next, the chips are packaged into bags. Now they can be sent to warehouses and stores.

Thanks to the potato farmers and the potato chip factory workers, you have a bag of crispy potato chips to snack on. Munch! Munch! So tasty!

WHERE ARE THE MOST POTATOES GROWN?

MAP KEY

🥔 Top potato growing areas

GLOSSARY

fertilizer A substance that makes soil richer and helps crops grow better.

GPS A system that quickly finds the exact location of an object. GPS stands for global positioning system.

harvester A machine that picks up potatoes and puts them in a truck.

humidity The measurement of moisture that is in the air.

inspect To look at something closely and carefully.

windrower A machine that digs up potatoes and lays them in rows.

WEBSITES

Idaho Potato Commission: Kids Zone
https://idahopotato.com/kids
Enjoy fun activities, recipes, and games to learn more about potatoes.

Meet the Potato Pals
https://www.potatoes.com/potatokids
Games, recipes, and educational resources from the Washington State Potato Commission help you learn more about potatoes.

Ontario Potato Board: Growing a Potato
https://www.ontariopotatoes.ca/growing-a-potato
Grow your own potato with a grown-up's help.

Every effort has been made to ensure that these websites are appropriate for children. However, because of the nature of the Internet, it is impossible to guarantee that these sites will remain active indefinitely or that their contents will not be altered.

READ MORE

Brundle, Harriet. *The Path of Potatoes.* Minneapolis: Bearport Publishing Company, 2022.

Neuenfeldt, Elizabeth. *Potato to French Fry.* Minneapolis: Bellwether Media, 2021.

Wallace, Elise. *In the Mood for Food.* Minneapolis: Lerner Publications, 2025.